Cakes

delicious recipes for all occasions

Yasa Boga

Marshall Cavendish
Cuisine

Translation by Ilona Pitt
Design by Steven Tan
Photographs by Soerjanto Photography, except for pages 79, 100 and 103
by Elements By The Box

Published by Marshall Cavendish Cuisine
An imprint of Marshall Cavendish International

Other Marshall Cavendish Offices:
Marshall Cavendish International. PO Box 65829, London, EC1P 1NY, UK • Marshall
Cavendish Corporation, 99 White Plains Road, Tarrytown NY 10591-9001, USA •
Marshall Cavendish International (Thailand) Co Ltd. 253 Asoke, 12th Flr, Sukhumvit
21 Road, Klongtoey Nua, Wattana, Bangkok 10110, Thailand • Marshall Cavendish
(Malaysia) Sdn Bhd, Times Subang, Lot 46, Subang Hi-Tech Industrial Park, Batu Tiga,
40000 Shah Alam, Selangor Darul Ehsan, Malaysia

Marshall Cavendish is a trademark of Times Publishing Limited

National Library Board, Singapore Cataloguing-in-Publication Data

Yasa Boga (Group)
Cakes :¬ delicious recipes for all occasions /¬ Yasa Boga. – Singapore : Marshall
Cavendish
Cuisine,¬ c2010.
p. cm. – (Home cooking)
ISBN-13 : 978-981-4302-26-5

1. Cake. I. Title. II. Series: Home cooking.

TX771
641.8653 – dc22   OCN639736383

Printed in Malaysia by Times Offset (M) Sdn Bhd

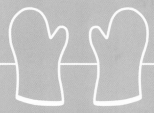

contents

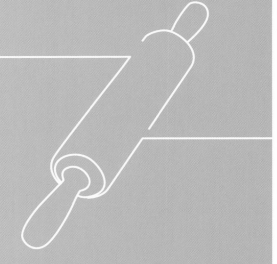

introduction

The cake recipes in this book are relatively easy to follow. All of them use basic ingredients that are readily available in supermarkets. For beginners in baking, we have provided some essential information on cake-making, including tips on ingredients, utensils and baking techniques, and some pointers for success. Once you're familiar with the basic steps and techniques, success will be just around the corner and baking cakes will be a breeze.

In this cookbook, we have included recipes for sponge cakes that do not require butter, margarine or oil at all, and some recipes where the amount of shortening is minimal or almost negligible. In Indonesia, these cakes are known as *taart* or Dutch-style cakes. Compared to butter cakes or regular cakes which are rich and moist due to their high fat content, *taart* cakes have a drier texture and so require cream as frosting for moisture.

basic ingredients

Flour

Sponge cakes require flour with medium protein content. Flour with medium protein content (plain/all-purpose flour) is ideal for the sponge cakes in this book because the cakes do not turn out too dense. When making butter cakes or cakes with a medium content of shortening (margarine/butter/oil), use low-protein flour (cake flour) which will absorb fat and moisture more quickly to give the cake a richer and finer texture.

Sugar

Use a fine grain castor (superfine) sugar for a fine-textured cake. If unavailable, use regular sugar, but pulse in a food processor briefly before using. Icing (confectioner's) sugar is normally used for decorative purposes and not directly in cakes. This soft, powdery sugar has anti-congealing properties and contains 3 per cent corn flour (cornstarch).

Butter

Butter helps to aerate and tenderise cakes. When whisked, its fat structure breaks into tiny fat particles which combine well with flour. Unsalted butter is recommended for cakes as it produces the best flavour by helping to better release the flavours of other ingredients. Produced from cow's milk, butter also provides a more luxurious aroma and taste compared to margarine. Before whisking with other ingredients, leave butter at room temperature to soften.

Eggs

Eggs help to aerate the cake and keep it moist and crisp. When whisked, the egg proteins create air bubbles which progressively become larger, assisting the cake mixture to expand when baked. Choose fresh free range eggs that weigh about 50 g ($1^2/_3$ oz) each. Always use eggs at room temperature. If eggs are chilled, leave them at room temperature for about 30 minutes before use.

Baking Powder and Bicarbonate of Soda

These chemical raising agents have the ability to enlarge air bubbles that form in the cake mixture during baking and prevent them from bursting. Air bubbles are important to help the cake to gain sufficient volume. Sift before measuring, especially bicarbonate of soda, which tends to clump.

Cake Stabilisers (TBM, VX, SP and Ovalet)

Also known as cake stabilisers, these emulsifying ingredients are additives which are commonly used by cake manufacturers to reduce the need for eggs and enable cakes to rise perfectly. It is necessary to add a little water when using TBM and VX, but it is not needed for Ovalet and SP.

All the cake recipes in this book do not require emulsifying ingredients. But if you would like to try using them, apply the measurement below as a guide:

200 g (7 oz) flour + 3 eggs + 1 tsp TBM + $^1/_4$ tsp VX + $3^1/_2$ Tbsp fluid (water/milk)

baking equipment

Electric Mixer

How long should one whisk a cake mixture for? Apart from varying amounts of ingredients in each recipe, your cake mixer capacity also plays a role in determining how long this will take. Logically, a 100-watt cake mixer will work slower than a 350-watt mixer. Instead of noting the amount of time needed, it is better to be observant and make sure that the mixture reaches its desired state as described in the recipe.

Baking Tin

When making a steamed sponge cake, use a perforated baking tin lined with baking paper to ensure that the cake does not crack on the surface. However, if you are making a steamed sponge cake that needs to be rolled or layered with filling, a normal baking tin will suffice.

For all the other types of cakes in this cookbook, regular baking tins will also suffice. However, be prudent and choose a plain tin, preferably a stainless steel one; tins made from shiny metals such as aluminum conduct heat too quickly and may cause the sides of the cake to cook much faster, resulting in the cake becoming dry at the edges.

Baking Paper

Lining the bottom and sides of the baking tin with baking paper will help you in unmoulding the cake easily when it is done. Measure and cut the baking paper according to the shape of the tin. Allow the paper lining the sides of the tin to extend above the sides by about 2-cm (1-in). Grease the baking paper with some butter or margarine to enable it to stick to the inside of the tin or tray and prevent it from falling into the batter when you are pouring it in.

Oven

Besides using an electric or gas oven, the cakes in this book can also be baked in a portable oven with equally satisfying results. When using a portable oven, the cake should be placed directly over the heat so that it is well distributed to enable even baking. Likewise, for a gas or an electric oven, the cake tin should always be placed in the centre of the middle rack so that heat is evenly distributed.

Electric ovens tend to have irregular heat distribution, causing cakes to rise in an uneven manner. If possible, recalibrate your oven temperature.

Gas ovens produce debris that can block the heat outlets if left to accumulate. If the oven is not hot enough, the cake will be undercooked. Therefore the heat outlets of the oven should be cleaned regularly to ensure that the oven operates at an optimum level.

baking techniques

Whisking

When making sponge cakes, eggs and sugar must be whisked into a thickened mixture that flows downwards in thick ribbons when the mixer whisks are lifted up. This shows that the whisking process has been done perfectly. Butter used for whisking has to be cut into small pieces and softened at room temperature for 15–20 minutes before combining it with sugar. The butter and sugar mixture should be whisked until thick and pale in colour. When adding eggs to butter, add them one by one while whisking, until the mixture is thick and well combined. Be careful not to over-whisk the mixture. When over-mixed, the mixture will be grainy. When baking, the cake will rise well at first but will sink in the centre shortly after rising, and have an extremely tough, dry and porous texture.

Folding

When making cakes, flour and other powdered ingredients should be sifted 2–3 times to remove lumps. They should be added in small batches to the whisked mixture of butter, sugar and eggs and folded in with a wooden spoon or rubber spatula.

To fold flour into a whisked mixture, make a 'cut' down middle of the mixture in a direction coming towards you with a wooden spoon or rubber spatula, then flip the spoon or spatula outwards towards the edges of the mixing bowl. Do this several times until mixture is just well-combined. With this method, the flour and whisked mixture will combine faster and also incorporate air, which ensures that the cake rises well. Do not fold in the flour for too long a time, but just enough for the flour to 'disappear' into the creamed mixture.

Adding Melted Fat to Cake Batter

Pour the fat into the cake batter in at least three small batches while folding continuously.

Filling the Cake Tin

When pouring cake batter into a cake tin, fill just half or two-thirds of the tin (do not fill the tin right to the brim). If the tin is filled to the brim, the batter will spill over in the oven while the cake is being baked. After filling the tin, gently smoothen the surface of the batter with the back of a metal spoon. To prevent the middle of the cake from forming a peak or cracking, make a slight dent in the middle of the batter with the back of a spoon.

Baking

Ensure that the oven is preheated for 10–15 minutes, and that the thermostat is set to the temperature recommended by the recipe when you are about to whisk the ingredients. Also make sure that the oven rack that the tin is going to be placed on is already in position.

Observe the baking process without opening the oven door. When the recommended baking time is about to end, you can open the oven door to test the cake's doneness by piercing its centre with a skewer. If the skewer comes out clean with no batter on it, the cake is ready. Check the cake sides too; if the sides look dry and have shrunk from the sides of the tin, this is an indication that the cake can be removed from the oven.

Removing the Cake from the Tin

Unmould baked cakes by inverting the cake tin onto a large flat plate or chopping board lined with baking paper. Carefully turn it the right side up by flipping it again. Place on a wire rack and leave to cool.

Assembling the Layered Cake

If you are able to master the skill, dividing a cake into two equal parts can be done easier with a thin, strong thread than a knife. However, measure the cake and mark the round first by 'walking' the thread around the cake to ensure that the cake is halved perfectly.

Filling or frosting should only be spread on the surface of the baked cake when it has completely cooled after taking it out of the oven.

When assembling layered cakes, press lightly on each cake layer after spreading the filling to ensure that they stick together. Use a sharp knife to trim and neaten the sides and edges of the cake.

Melting Chocolate

When melting chocolate, use a double boiler. If you do not have one, place the chopped pieces of chocolate in a bowl that can sit on the top of a saucepan of simmering water without the bottom of the bowl touching the water. Stir until the chocolate has melted completely.

Making Buttercream

Buttercream is made of whisked butter, sugar and eggs and is used as a filling as well as a frosting for cakes. If using only egg whites, the buttercream will taste lighter. Adding melted chocolate or mocha paste to the buttercream will help enhance its aroma and taste.

Egg Yolk Buttercream
3 egg yolks
5 Tbsp water
125 g (4^1/$_2$ oz) castor (superfine) sugar
225 g (8 oz) unsalted butter

- Whisk egg yolks until thick and pale in colour.
- Heat water and sugar in a pot over medium heat and stir until sugar is completely dissolved. Gradually pour syrup into egg yolk mixture while whisking constantly, until mixture has thickened.
- In a separate mixing bowl, whisk butter until softened. Gradually add egg yolk and sugar mixture, whisking constantly at low speed until a soft, creamy consistency is achieved.

Egg White Buttercream
1 egg white
5 Tbsp water
125 g (4$^1/_2$ oz) castor (superfine) sugar
225 g (8 oz) unsalted butter

- Whisk egg white until stiff peaks form. Set aside.
- In the meantime, heat water and sugar in a pot over medium heat. Stir mixture until sugar is completely dissolved.
- While sugar syrup is still hot, gradually pour into egg white mixture while whisking constantly, until mixture has thickened. Set aside.
- In a separate mixing bowl, whisk butter until softened, then gradually add egg white and sugar mixture, whisking constantly at low speed until a soft creamy consistency is achieved. Refrigerate and chill if not using immediately.

Decorating the Cake

There are times when cakes are coated with frosting such as icing (confectioner's) sugar, royal icing, melted chocolate or buttercream. The objective is to make the cake more attractive, in addition to enriching the taste of the cake. These are some simple decoration techniques:

Icing (Confectioner's) Sugar

Cut baking paper into 1–2 cm ($^1/_2$–1 in) wide strips and arrange on the surface of the cake to form a pattern. Sift the icing sugar over the cake and remove the paper strips carefully to leave a pattern on the cake.

Royal Icing

Ready-made royal icing is available from baking specialty shops. If you prefer homemade royal icing, here is a recipe:

225 g (8 oz) icing (confectioner's) sugar
1 egg white
$^1/_4$ tsp cream of tartar
1–2 tsp lime juice
a few drops food colouring of choice

- With an electric mixer, whisk all ingredients except lime juice and food colouring until thick and doubled in volume. Add lime juice and food colouring. Stir to mix well before using.

Royal icing is more suitable for regular cakes or butter cakes as it is quite dry compared to buttercream. Spread it all over the cake evenly with a spatula. Put the remaining icing in a piping bag fitted with a patterned nozzle. Pipe the icing onto the surface of the cake to form desired patterns. If icing becomes a little dry, simply add a little more lime juice and mix until it is of a consistency that can be piped.

Chocolate Ganache
Melt 100 g ($3^1/_2$ oz) chopped baking chocolate and 1 tsp butter together. Place the cake on a wire rack in a baking tray. Slowly pour the melted chocolate on top of the cake until the cake is covered with ganache.

Chocolate Frosting and Filling
100 g ($3^1/_2$ oz) chopped cooking chocolate
50 g ($1^2/_3$ oz) cocoa powder
8 Tbsp water
280 g (10 oz) castor (superfine) sugar

- Combine ingredients in a saucepan over low heat. Stir until mixture is combined, thickened and glazed. Spread onto the cake with a spatula or a palette knife immediately, as the chocolate mixture will harden when cooled.

Buttercream
Similar to royal icing, buttercream can be used as cake frosting with the assistance of a spatula and piping bag. Do not be afraid to be creative; although buttercream can be applied on regular butter cakes, it may be too rich when paired with heavy, buttery cakes. It is more suitable for lighter sponge cakes which contain little or no fat.

Storing Cakes
Cakes without frosting or filling can be kept for 1–2 months in the freezer. Wrap tightly with plastic wrap and store in an airtight container before putting in the freezer. Defrost cake to room temperature before cutting or decorating.

weights and measures

Quantities for this book are given in Metric, Imperial and American (spoon) measures. Standard spoon and cup measurements used are: 1 tsp = 5 ml, 1 Tbsp = 15 ml, 1 cup = 250 ml. All measures are level unless otherwise stated.

LIQUID AND VOLUME MEASURES

Metric	Imperial	American
5 ml	$1/6$ fl oz	1 teaspoon
10 ml	$1/3$ fl oz	1 dessertspoon
15 ml	$1/2$ fl oz	1 tablespoon
60 ml	2 fl oz	$1/4$ cup (4 tablespoons)
85 ml	$2^1/2$ fl oz	$1/4$ cup
90 ml	3 fl oz	$3/8$ cup (6 tablespoons)
125 ml	4 fl oz	$1/2$ cup
180 ml	6 fl oz	$3/4$ cup
250 ml	8 fl oz	1 cup
300 ml	10 fl oz ($1/2$ pint)	$1^1/4$ cups
375 ml	12 fl oz	$1^1/2$ cups
435 ml	14 fl oz	$1^3/4$ cups
500 ml	16 fl oz	2 cups
625 ml	20 fl oz (1 pint)	$2^1/2$ cups
750 ml	24 fl oz ($1^1/5$ pints)	3 cups
1 litre	32 fl oz ($1^3/5$ pints)	4 cups
1.25 litres	40 fl oz (2 pints)	5 cups
1.5 litres	48 fl oz ($2^2/5$ pints)	6 cups
2.5 litres	80 fl oz (4 pints)	10 cups

DRY MEASURES

Metric	Imperial
30 grams	1 ounce
45 grams	$1^1/2$ ounces
55 grams	2 ounces
70 grams	$2^1/2$ ounces
85 grams	3 ounces
100 grams	$3^1/2$ ounces
110 grams	4 ounces
125 grams	$4^1/2$ ounces
140 grams	5 ounces
280 grams	10 ounces
450 grams	16 ounces (1 pound)
500 grams	1 pound, $1^1/2$ ounces
700 grams	$1^1/2$ pounds
800 grams	$1^3/4$ pounds
1 kilogram	2 pounds, 3 ounces
1.5 kilograms	3 pounds, $4^1/2$ ounces
2 kilograms	4 pounds, 6 ounces

OVEN TEMPERATURE

	°C	°F	Gas Regulo
Very slow	120	250	1
Slow	150	300	2
Moderately slow	160	325	3
Moderate	180	350	4
Moderately hot	190/200	370/400	5/6
Hot	210/220	410/440	6/7
Very hot	230	450	8
Super hot	250/290	475/550	9/10

LENGTH

Metric	Imperial
0.5 cm	$1/4$ inch
1 cm	$1/2$ inch
1.5 cm	$3/4$ inch
2.5 cm	1 inch

rainbowcake

Butter for greasing tin

6 eggs

250 g (9 oz) castor (superfine) sugar

2 tsp vanilla extract or $^1/_2$ tsp ground vanilla

275 g (9$^1/_2$ oz) cake flour, sifted

200 ml (6$^1/_2$ fl oz / $^4/_5$ cup) coconut milk from $^1/_4$ fresh coconut or 4 Tbsp packaged coconut cream + 4 Tbsp water

3 drops red food colouring

3 drops green food colouring

- Preheat steamer over medium heat. Prepare a 20 x 7-cm (8 x 3-in) round tin. Grease tin with butter and line with baking paper or grease tin with butter and sprinkle with flour. Set aside.

- With an electric mixer, whisk eggs, sugar and vanilla until mixture is thick and pale in colour. Using a rubber spatula, gradually fold flour and coconut milk in small amounts into egg mixture, mixing well at each turn.

- Divide cake mixture into three equal parts. Stir red food colouring into one part and green food colouring into another part.

- Pour one ladle of green-coloured mixture into prepared tin and steam for 5–10 minutes. Repeat step with red-coloured mixture, followed by the original mixture, until all three parts of cake mixture have been used up.

- Steam cake for another 15 minutes or until a skewer inserted into the centre of cake comes out clean. Remove cake to a wire rack and leave to cool before serving.

pandancustardroll

Butter for greasing tin

Cake

3 eggs + 1 egg yolk

100 g (3¹/₂ oz) castor (superfine) sugar

100 g (3¹/₂ oz) plain (all-purpose) flour + ¹/₄ tsp baking powder, sifted

3 Tbsp packaged coconut cream + 1¹/₂ tsp suji leaf water or green food colouring

Custard

125 ml (4 fl oz / ¹/₂ cup) coconut cream

1 Tbsp rice flour

2 Tbsp corn flour (cornstarch)

125 g (4¹/₂ oz) grated palm sugar, sliced thinly

1 Tbsp castor (superfine) sugar

A pinch of salt

1 egg yolk, whisked

- Preheat steamer over medium heat. Grease a 20 x 20 x 3-cm (8 x 8 x 1-in) square tin with butter and line with baking paper. Set aside.

- Prepare custard. Mix all ingredients except for egg yolk together in a saucepan. Stir constantly over low heat until custard coats the back of a wooden spoon. Stir egg yolk into mixture quickly and remove from heat. Allow mixture to cool while stirring occasionally.

- Prepare cake. Whisk eggs and sugar with an electric mixer until mixture is thick and almost doubled in volume. Using a rubber spatula, gradually fold flour and baking powder, coconut cream and suji leaf water or colouring in small amounts into egg mixture, mixing well after each turn.

- Pour mixture into tin and place tin in steamer. Steam until cake is done. This will take 20–30 minutes depending on the level of heat. Remove from steamer and invert onto a clean tea towel. Lay another clean tea towel on a flat surface and gently flip cake onto it so that it faces the right side up.

- Spread an even layer of custard over cake. While cake is still hot, roll it up tightly, using the tea towel it is placed on to compact it. Wrap cake with tea towel and leave aside for 30 minutes before cutting as desired.

NOTE:

Before steaming, wrap a tea towel over the inside of the steamer lid to prevent moisture from dripping onto the cake mixture.

Always make sure that the water in the steamer is sufficient, and that it is simmering before placing the cake mixture in to steam.

steamedmoskovis

Butter for greasing tin

Cake

7 egg yolks

2 egg whites

200 g (7 oz) castor (superfine) sugar

175 g (6 oz) plain (all-purpose) flour +
$^1/_2$ tsp baking powder, sifted

100 ml (3$^1/_2$ fl oz / $^2/_5$ cup) evaporated
milk or 5 Tbsp water + 2 Tbsp milk powder

Mixed Fruit

200 g (7 oz) red and green glacé
cherries, cut into 0.5-cm ($^1/_4$-in) cubes

100 g (3$^1/_2$ oz) candied citrus peel,
cut into 0.5-cm ($^1/_4$-in) slices

200 g (7 oz) raisins

6 Tbsp rum

- Preheat steamer over medium heat. Prepare a 20 x 20 x 7-cm (8 x 8 x 3-in) square tin. Grease tin with butter and sprinkle with flour. Set aside.

- Prepare mixed fruit. Put cherries, citrus peel, raisins and rum in a large bowl and mix well. Set aside.

- Prepare cake. Whisk egg yolks, egg whites and sugar with an electric mixer at low speed for 1–2 minutes, then increase mixer speed and whisk for about 10 minutes until mixture is thick and pale in colour.

- Using a rubber spatula, gradually fold flour and milk in small amounts into egg mixture, mixing well at each turn.

- Pour one-third of batter into cake tin. Level batter and steam for about 10 minutes. Sprinkle one-third of mixed fruit on top of cake and pour another one-third of cake batter on top and steam for another 10 minutes.

- Repeat step above with remaining cake batter and another one-third of mixed fruit. Steam for 5 minutes, then sprinkle remaining mixed fruit on top. Steam for another 15 minutes until a skewer inserted into the centre of cake comes out clean. Leave to cool and cut as desired.

zebracake

Butter for greasing tin

5 Tbsp packaged coconut milk

5 Tbsp boiled water

5 egg yolks

3 egg whites

250 g (9 oz) castor (superfine) sugar

1/2 tsp ground vanilla or vanilla extract

200 g (7 oz) cake flour

1–2 Tbsp store-bought chocolate paste

- Preheat steamer over high heat. Prepare a round tin 20-cm (8-in) in diameter. Grease tin with butter and line with baking paper, then grease again and sprinkle with flour. Set aside.

- Mix coconut milk and water together and stir well. Set aside.

- With an electric mixer, whisk eggs, sugar and vanilla at low speed for 30 seconds. Increase speed to high and whisk until mixture is thick and almost doubled in volume. Using a rubber spatula, gradually fold flour and coconut milk in small amounts into egg mixture, mixing well at each turn.

- Divide cake mixture into 2 equal parts. Add chocolate paste to one part and mix well.

- Slowly pour a ladle of chocolate cake mixture into centre of tin, followed by a ladle of plain cake mixture directly on top. The layers of cake mixtures will spread slowly. Continue to ladle cake mixtures into tin alternately until both mixtures have been used up.

- Steam for 20–25 minutes until a skewer inserted into the centre of cake comes out clean. Remove from tin and leave to cool. Cut and serve as desired.

steamedbrownies

Butter for greasing tin

Cake

150 ml (5$^{1}/_{3}$ fl oz) milk

50 g (1$^{2}/_{3}$ oz) cocoa powder

3 eggs

225 g (8 oz) castor (superfine) sugar

100 g (3$^{1}/_{2}$ oz) cake flour +
$^{1}/_{2}$ tsp baking powder, sifted

Chocolate Cream Filling

1 tsp butter

5 Tbsp milk

150 g (5$^{1}/_{3}$oz) dark cooking
chocolate, melted

- Preheat steamer over medium heat. Prepare a 20 x 20 x 6-cm (8 x 8 x 2$^{1}/_{2}$-in) square tin. Grease tin with butter and line with baking paper. Set aside.

- Prepare cake. Heat milk to boiling point. Add cocoa powder and stir until completely dissolved. Remove from heat and leave to cool. With an electric mixer, whisk eggs and sugar in until mixture is thick and almost doubled in volume.

- Using a rubber spatula, gradually fold flour and chocolate milk in small amounts into egg mixture, mixing gently at each turn.

- Pour mixture into prepared tin and steam until a skewer inserted into the centre of cake comes out clean. This will take 20–30 minutes, depending on the level of heat. Remove cake from tin and leave to cool.

- Prepare chocolate cream filling. Add butter to milk in a small pot and bring to boil. Remove from heat. Add melted chocolate and stir until mixture thickens to a spreadable consistency.

- To assemble cake, halve cake horizontally into 2 layers. Spread chocolate cream filling evenly on surface of bottom layer, then replace top layer and press down firmly but lightly so the cakes stick together. To decorate cake (optional), cut strips of paper and place on top of cake. Sift icing sugar over and remove paper. Cut and serve as desired.

chickenandcheese
layercake

Butter for greasing tin

Cake

3 eggs

100 g (3$^{1}/_{2}$ oz) castor (superfine) sugar

200 g (7 oz) cake flour + $^{1}/_{2}$ tsp baking powder, sifted

3 Tbsp milk

$^{1}/_{4}$ tsp salt

Chicken and Cheese Mixture

1 Tbsp margarine

$^{1}/_{2}$ onion, peeled and roughly chopped

2 cloves garlic, peeled and finely chopped

200 g (7 oz) boiled chicken, skinned and diced

$^{1}/_{4}$ tsp ground pepper

$^{1}/_{4}$ tsp ground nutmeg

2 Tbsp chopped spring onions (scallions)

100 g (3$^{1}/_{2}$ oz) grated cheddar cheese

- Prepare chicken and cheese mixture. Heat margarine in a pan and stir-fry onion and garlic until fragrant. Add chicken and season with pepper and nutmeg. Continue to stir-fry for 1 minute. Remove and set aside to cool. Sprinkle with spring onions.

- Preheat steamer over low heat. Prepare a 22 x 22 x 7-cm (8$^{1}/_{2}$ x 8$^{1}/_{2}$ x 3-in) square tin. Grease tin with butter and line with baking paper, then grease again. Set aside.

- Prepare cake. Whisk eggs and sugar with an electric mixer until mixture is thick and almost doubled in volume. Using a rubber spatula, gradually fold flour in small amounts into egg mixture, mixing well at each turn. Add milk and salt and mix well. Pour half of mixture into prepared tin.

- Steam for 10 minutes until cake is half-cooked. Remove from heat and top with an even layer of chicken mixture. Sprinkle grated cheese all over.

- Gently pour remaining mixture into tin and return to steamer for about 20 minutes until a skewer inserted into the centre of cake comes out clean. Remove from tin and leave to cool. Cut and serve as desired.

corned beef layer cake

Butter for greasing tin

Cake

6 eggs

100 g (3 1/2 oz) castor (superfine) sugar

200 g (7 oz) cake flour + 1/2 tsp baking powder, sifted

3 Tbsp milk

Corned Beef Mixture

1 Tbsp margarine

1/4 onion, peeled and roughly chopped

2 cloves garlic, peeled and finely chopped

180 g (6 1/2 oz) corned beef

100 g (3 1/2 oz) green peas

1/4 tsp ground pepper

1/4 tsp ground nutmeg

- Prepare corned beef mixture. Heat margarine in a pan and stir-fry onion and garlic until fragrant. Stir in corned beef and green peas. Season with pepper and nutmeg. Continue to stir-fry for 1 minute. Remove and set aside to cool.

- Preheat steamer over low heat. Prepare a 20 x 20 x 7-cm (8 x 8 x 3-in) square tin. Grease tin with butter and line with baking paper, then grease again. Set aside.

- Prepare cake. Whisk eggs and sugar with an electric mixer until mixture is thick and almost doubled in volume. Using a rubber spatula, gradually fold flour in small amounts into egg mixture, mixing well at each turn. Add in milk and mix well. Pour half of mixture into prepared tin.

- Steam for 10 minutes until cake is half-cooked. Remove from heat and top with an even layer of corned beef mixture.

- Gently pour remaining mixture into tin and return to steamer for about 20 minutes until a skewer inserted into the centre of cake comes out clean. Remove from tin and leave to cool. Cut and serve as desired.

steamed young
coconut cake

Butter for greasing tin

1–2 young coconuts, flesh scraped out and shredded; shells discarded

6 eggs

100 g (3$^{1}/_{2}$ oz) sugar

125 g (4$^{1}/_{2}$ oz) grated palm sugar, chopped

$^{1}/_{2}$ tsp vanilla extract

200 g (7 oz) plain (all-purpose) flour + $^{1}/_{2}$ tsp baking powder, sifted

125 ml (4 fl oz / $^{1}/_{2}$ cup) packaged coconut cream

1–2 drops pandan extract

- Preheat steamer. Prepare about 20 small ramekins, each 5–6-cm (2–2$^{1}/_{2}$-in) in diameter. Grease ramekins with butter and spoon 1–2 Tbsp shredded coconut flesh into each ramekin. Set aside.

- With an electric mixer, whisk eggs, sugar, palm sugar and vanilla extract until mixture is thick and almost doubled in volume. Using a rubber spatula, gradually fold flour, coconut cream and pandan extract in small amounts into egg mixture, mixing well at each turn.

- Divide mixture equally among ramekins. Place in preheated steamer and steam for about 15 minutes until cakes are done. Remove from ramekins and leave to cool. Garnish as desired and serve.

blackforestroll

Cake

12 egg yolks

4 egg whites

1 tsp vanilla extract or $1/4$ tsp ground vanilla

150 g ($5^1/3$ oz) castor (superfine) sugar

60 g (2 oz) cake flour

25 g ($^3/4$ oz) cocoa powder

100 g ($3^1/2$ oz) butter, whisked until soft + more for greasing tin

$3^1/4$ Tbsp black cherry juice

$2^1/4$ Tbsp cherry liqueur (Kirschwasser) or rum, or 1 Tbsp rum extract

Cream and Fruit Filling

500 ml (16 fl oz / 2 cups) non-dairy whipping cream

60 g (2 oz) icing (confectioner's) sugar

220 g (8 oz) canned black cherries, drained and halved

Decoration

100 g ($3^1/2$ oz) dark cooking chocolate, grated into slivers

- Preheat oven to 190°C (370°F). Prepare a 30 x 30 x 3-cm (12 x 12 x 1-in) square tin. Grease tin with butter and line with baking paper, then grease again. Set aside.

- Prepare cake. Whisk egg yolks, egg whites, vanilla and sugar with an electric mixer until thick and pale in colour. Using a rubber spatula, gradually fold flour and cocoa powder into egg mixture in a single direction until combined. Gently and gradually fold in butter until combined. Pour mixture into prepared tin and level surface.

- Place tin in preheated oven and bake for about 25 minutes until a skewer inserted into the centre of cake comes out clean. Remove cake from tin and place on a large sheet of baking paper.

- Mix cherry juice and liqueur together. Sprinkle all over surface of cake.

- Prepare cream and fruit filling. Whisk whipping cream with icing sugar with an electric mixer until thick. Spread half of whipped cream evenly on surface of cake, then top with cherry halves. While cake is still hot, roll it up tightly, using the baking paper it is placed on to compact it. Wrap cake in baking paper and refrigerate until sufficiently chilled.

- To decorate cake, spread remaining whipped cream evenly all over surface of cake roll and sprinkle with slivers of grated chocolate.

vanilla**cake**with**cheese**

Vanilla Cake

5 eggs

125 g (4$\frac{1}{2}$ oz) castor (superfine) sugar

$\frac{1}{4}$ tsp ground vanilla or vanilla extract

125 g (4$\frac{1}{2}$ oz) plain (all-purpose flour) +
$\frac{1}{2}$ tsp baking powder, sifted

4 Tbsp cooking oil or melted butter +
more for greasing tin

Filling and Decoration

1 quantity buttercream (page 11)

200 g (7 oz) grated cheese

- Preheat oven to 170°C (330°F). Prepare a 20-cm (8-in) square tin or a 22-cm (8$\frac{1}{2}$-in) round tin. Grease tin with butter and line with baking paper, then grease again. Set aside.

- With an electric mixer, whisk eggs, sugar and vanilla until thick and almost doubled in volume. Using a rubber spatula, gradually fold flour in small amounts into egg mixture until just combined. Add oil or melted butter in small amounts and gently mix until combined. Pour mixture into prepared tin.

- Place tin in preheated oven and bake for about 35 minutes until a skewer inserted into the centre of cake comes out clean. Remove from tin and let cool.

- To assemble cake, halve cake horizontally into two layers. Spread buttercream evenly over bottom layer. Sprinkle half portion of cheese all over, then place top layer over and press down firmly but lightly.

- Frost cake with remaining buttercream. Sprinkle with remaining cheese and garnish as desired.

tiramisu

Cake

1 vanilla cake (page 33)

500 ml (16 fl oz / 2 cups) whipping cream, chilled

Cocoa powder for sprinkling

Coffee and Liqueur Syrup

150 ml (5 1/3 fl oz) water

2 Tbsp instant coffee granules

2 Tbsp castor (superfine) sugar

3 Tbsp coffee liqueur (Tia Maria/ Kahlua/Bailey's) or rum

Cheese Mixture

150 g (5 1/3 oz) castor (superfine) sugar + 5 Tbsp water

3 egg yolks

2 Tbsp gelatin powder + 3 Tbsp water

250 g (9 oz) mascarpone cheese, chilled

- Prepare vanilla cake according to directions on page 33.

- Prepare coffee and liqueur syrup. Bring water to boil. Add instant coffee and sugar and stir until dissolved. Remove from heat and leave to cool. Stir in coffee liqueur. Set aside.

- Prepare cheese mixture. Simmer sugar mixture over low heat until sugar has dissolved and mixture is the consistency of syrup. Do not stir, but occasionally swirl saucepan. With an electric mixer, whisk egg yolks until pale in colour. Add hot sugar syrup and continue to whisk until mixture is almost doubled in volume and white in colour. Leave to cool.

- Heat gelatin powder and water mixture until gelatin has dissolved completely. Set aside. Add mascarpone cheese to cooled egg yolk mixture and whisk until well combined. Add a little bit of cheese mixture into dissolved gelatin and mix evenly. Add gelatin mixture to cheese mixture and stir until well combined.

- To assemble cakes, prepare 10 plastic strips each 12 x 8-cm (5 x 3-in). Seal each strip with adhesive tape to form mini cake rings. Halve vanilla cake horizontally and cut out 20 cake rounds using cake rings. Brush surface of each cake round with coffee and liqueur syrup. Put one cake round (brushed surface facing up) into each cake ring to serve as bases.

- With an electric mixer, beat whipping cream until thick. Gently add whipped cream in small amounts into cheese mixture. Scoop 1 Tbsp cream and cheese mixture into each plastic cake ring and top with another cake round (brushed surfaces touching cream and cheese mixture). Finally, brush top of each cake with cream and cheese mixture. Pipe remaining cheese mixture over cakes if desired and sprinkle with cocoa powder.

ontbytkoek

3 eggs + 2 egg yolks

75 g (2²/₃ oz) grated palm sugar

50 g (1²/₃ oz) castor (superfine) sugar

100 g (3¹/₂ oz) plain (all-purpose) flour + ¹/₄ tsp ground cinnamon + ¹/₄ tsp ground mixed spices, sifted

3 Tbsp melted butter + more for greasing tin

1 Tbsp sliced almonds, optional

- Preheat oven to 175°C (340°F). Prepare two 18–20-cm (7–8-in) loaf tins, about 5–6-cm (2–2¹/₂-in) high. Grease tins with butter and line with baking paper, then grease again. Set aside.

- With an electric mixer, whisk eggs, palm sugar and sugar until thick and almost doubled in volume. Using a rubber spatula, gradually fold flour in small amounts into egg mixture until just combined. Gradually add melted butter and gently mix until combined. Pour mixture into prepared tins. Sprinkle with sliced almonds if desired.

- Place tins apart in preheated oven and bake for about 45 minutes until cakes are done. Remove from tins and leave to cool.

mochacake

Cake

4 eggs

100 g (3¹/₂ oz) castor (superfine) sugar

¹/₂ tsp mocha paste

100 g (3¹/₂ oz) cake flour

60 g (2 oz) butter, melted + more for greasing tin

Filling and Frosting

2 tsp instant coffee granules dissolved in 1 Tbsp hot water

1 quantity buttercream (page 11)

Syrup

100 g (3¹/₂ oz) castor (superfine) sugar + 100 ml (3¹/₂ fl oz / ³/₈ cup) water

1¹/₂ Tbsp coffee liqueur (Bailey's/ Kahlua/Tia Maria) or rum

Decoration

75 g (2²/₃ oz) fried cashew nuts, roughly chopped

75 g (2²/₃ oz) dark cooking chocolate, melted

- Preheat oven to 175°C (350°F). Prepare a 20-cm (8-in) diameter round tin. Grease tin with butter and line with baking paper, then grease again. Set aside.

- Prepare filling and frosting. Add coffee mixture to buttercream and whisk until combined. Set aside.

- Prepare syrup. Heat sugar and water solution until sugar has completely dissolved, then leave to cool to room temperature. Stir in coffee liqueur or rum. Set aside.

- Prepare cake. Whisk eggs, sugar and mocha paste with an electric mixer until thick and almost doubled in volume. Using a rubber spatula, gradually fold flour in small amounts into egg mixture until just combined. Add melted butter in small amounts and gently mix until combined. Pour into prepared tin.

- Place tin in preheated oven and bake for about 35 minutes until a skewer inserted into the centre of cake comes out clean. Remove from tin and let cool.

- To assemble cake, halve cake horizontally into 2 layers. Sprinkle syrup on the surface of each layer. Spread buttercream evenly over bottom layer, then place top layer over and press down firmly but lightly so that they stick together. Frost cake all over with remaining buttercream. Press chopped nuts gently into sides of cake. Pipe melted chocolate over top of cake. If desired, pipe buttercream rosettes on cake and top with chocolate decorations.

birthday cake

16 egg yolks

6 egg whites

200 g (7 oz) castor (superfine) sugar

$^1/_2$ tsp ground vanilla or vanilla extract

200 g (7 oz) plain (all-purpose) flour +
2 Tbsp corn flour (cornstarch), sifted

90 g (3$^1/_4$ oz) butter, whisked until soft + more for
greasing tin

Rum as desired

2 quantities buttercream (page 11)

- Preheat oven to 180°C (350°F). Prepare a 24 x 24 x 6-cm (9$^1/_2$ x 9$^1/_2$ x 2$^1/_2$-in) square tin. Grease tin with butter and line with baking paper, then grease again. Set aside.

- With an electric mixer, whisk egg yolks, egg whites, sugar and vanilla until thick and almost doubled in volume. Using a rubber spatula, gradually fold flour mixture in small amounts into egg mixture until combined. Gradually add melted butter and gently mix until combined. Pour mixture into prepared tin.

- Place tin in preheated oven and bake for about 45 minutes until a skewer inserted into the centre of cake comes out clean. Remove from tin and leave to cool.

- To assemble cake, halve cake horizontally into 2 layers. Sprinkle rum on surface of each layer. Spread buttercream evenly over bottom layer, then place top layer over and press down firmly but lightly so that the layers stick together. Frost cake with remaining buttercream and decorate as desired before serving.

poundcake

Cake

450 g (1 lb) butter + more for greasing tin

1/2 tsp ground vanilla or vanilla extract

450 g (1 lb) castor (superfine) sugar

8 eggs

450 g (1 lb) plain (all-purpose) flour

Topping

150 g (5 1/3 oz) plain (all-purpose) flour, sifted

100 g (3 1/2 oz) butter, diced

100 g (3 1/2 oz) castor (superfine) sugar

- Preheat oven to 150°C (300°F). Prepare two 20 x 10-cm (8 x 4-in) loaf tins or a 24-cm (9 1/2-in) diameter kugelhopf bundt tin. Grease tins with butter and line with baking paper, then grease again. Set aside.

- Prepare topping. Mix all ingredients together and stir with a fork until grainy. Set aside.

- Prepare cake. Whisk butter, vanilla and sugar with an electric mixer until mixture is thick and pale in colour. Add eggs to mixture, one at a time and whisk until well combined. Using a rubber spatula, gradually fold flour in small amounts into egg mixture until combined.

- Pour mixture into prepared tin and level surface of mixture. If using loaf tins, make a slight hollow in the centre of batter with the back of a teaspoon. This will prevent the cake from cracking in the middle when baked. Sprinkle topping on top of batter.

- Place tins apart in preheated oven and bake for about 1 hour until tops of cakes are golden brown. Remove from tins and leave to cool.

madeleines

2 eggs, yolks and whites separated

50 g (1²/₃ oz) castor (superfine) sugar

2 Tbsp brown sugar or grated palm sugar

1¹/₂ Tbsp honey

90 g (3¹/₄ oz) plain (all-purpose) flour + 1 tsp baking powder + a pinch of salt, sifted

60 g (2 oz) unsalted butter, melted + more for greasing tin

Icing (confectioner's) sugar for sprinkling

- Preheat oven to 180°C (350°F). Grease a madeleine tray and refrigerate for about 10 minutes. Remove from fridge and grease once more. Keep refrigerated until required.

- With an electric mixer, beat egg yolks with half the castor sugar and brown or palm sugar and honey until mixture is thick and pale in colour. Using a clean and dry whisk, beat egg whites with remaining castor sugar until stiff peaks form. Fold one-third of egg white mixture into egg yolk mixture until combined.

- Using a rubber spatula, gradually and gently fold flour and remaining egg white mixture in alternate batches into egg yolk mixture until just combined. Finally, add melted butter and mix until just combined. Pour into chilled tray and set aside for 10 minutes.

- Place tray in preheated oven and bake for about 8 minutes until cakes are brown. Remove cakes from tray immediately and transfer to a wire rack to cool. Sprinkle with icing sugar before serving.

NOTE:

Originating from the town of Commercy in the Lorraine region of France, these small, delightful cakes have traditionally been baked in shell-shaped moulds. Moulds of other shapes can be used, provided that the width of each individual mould does not exceed 5-cm (2-in).

teabrack

Butter for greasing tin

2 black tea teabags

300 ml (10 fl oz / 1¼ cups) boiling water

250 g (9 oz) raisins

1 egg

2 Tbsp marmalade or pineapple jam

200 g (7 oz) brown sugar

275 g (9¾ oz) plain (all-purpose) flour

2 tsp baking powder, sifted

Icing (confectioner's) sugar for sprinkling, optional

- Steep tea bags in boiling water until a thick dark brew has formed. Remove and discard tea bags. When tea is no longer hot but still warm, add raisins to it. Store in a sealed container and leave to soak in the refrigerator.

- Preheat oven to 160°C (325°F). Prepare a 20 x 9-cm (8 x 3½-in) loaf tin or a 15-cm (6-in) heart-shaped tin. Grease tin with butter and line with baking paper, then grease again. Set aside.

- Drain raisins and place in a large mixing bowl. Add egg, marmalade or pineapple jam, brown sugar, flour and baking powder. With a wooden spoon, stir batter evenly until well combined. Pour batter into prepared tin and level with the back of a spoon.

- Place tin in preheated oven and bake for about 1½ hours until a skewer inserted into the centre of cake comes out clean. Remove cake from tin and leave to cool. Sprinkle with icing sugar to decorate, if desired.

NOTE:

The raisins in this recipe should be steeped in black tea overnight to best infuse them with the flavour of the tea. This simple cake is the perfect accompaniment to a cup of tea or coffee.

coconut milk and fermented cassava bluder

Butter for greasing tin

125 g (4^1/$_2$ oz) mature sweet fermented cassava

3 Tbsp packaged coconut cream

6 egg yolks

4 egg whites

100 g (3^1/$_2$ oz) castor (superfine) sugar

1 tsp vanilla extract or ^{1}/$_2$ tsp ground vanilla

100 g (3^1/$_2$ oz) plain (all-purpose) flour

75 g (2^2/$_3$ oz) butter, whisked until soft

50 g (1^2/$_3$ oz) chopped almonds

50 g (1^2/$_3$ oz) raisins, halved

- Preheat oven to 175°C (340°F). Prepare a 17 x 8 x 9-cm (6^1/$_2$ x 3 x 3^1/$_2$-in) loaf tin. Grease tin with butter and line with baking paper, then grease again. Set aside.

- In a large bowl, mix fermented cassava with coconut cream and mash with a fork until combined. Set aside.

- With an electric mixer, whisk egg yolks and whites, sugar and vanilla until mixture is thick and almost doubled in volume. Add mashed cassava to egg mixture and stir to mix well. Using a rubber spatula, gradually fold flour in small amounts into egg mixture until combined. Add whisked butter and mix until well combined. Pour mixture into prepared tin and level with the back of a spoon. Sprinkle almonds and raisins on top of cake.

- Place tin in preheated oven and bake for about 40 minutes until a skewer inserted into the centre of cake comes out clean. Leave cake in tin for about 5 minutes before removing to a wire rack to cool.

pandancustardcake

Cake

5 eggs

125 g (4½ oz) castor (superfine) sugar

¼ tsp ground vanilla

125 g (4½ oz) plain (all-purpose) flour

4 Tbsp cooking oil or melted butter + more for greasing tin

Pandan Custard

180 ml (6 fl oz / ¾ cup) coconut milk, strained from ¼ freshly grated coconut

2 Tbsp corn flour (cornstarch)

2 Tbsp plain (all-purpose) flour

1 tsp pandan paste

100 g (3½ oz) castor (superfine) sugar

3 egg yolks, lightly beaten

- Preheat oven to 175°C (340°F). Prepare a 20-cm (8-in) square tin or a 22-cm (8½-in) diameter round tin. Grease tin with butter and line with baking paper, then grease again. Set aside.

- Prepare pandan custard. Simmer coconut milk, corn flour, flour and pandan paste in a saucepan over low heat, stirring constantly until mixture turns thick. Add sugar and stir thoroughly until dissolved. Add 1 Tbsp hot coconut milk mixture to egg yolks and stir briefly, then return egg yolk mixture to saucepan. Cook briefly, stirring constantly. Remove saucepan from heat and leave to cool. While pandan custard is cooling, stir mixture occasionally to prevent a film from forming on surface.

- Prepare cake. Whisk eggs, sugar and vanilla with an electric mixer until thick and pale in colour. Using a rubber spatula, gradually and gently fold flour in small amounts into egg mixture until combined. Add cooking oil or melted butter in small amounts, stirring constantly until combined.

- Pour mixture into prepared tin. Place tin in preheated oven and bake for about 35 minutes until a skewer inserted into the centre of cake comes out clean. Remove cake from tin and leave to cool.

- To assemble cake, halve cake horizontally into 2 layers. Spread pandan custard evenly over bottom layer, then place top layer over and press down firmly but lightly so that layers stick together. Decorate as desired.

lamingtons

Cake

225 g (8 oz) butter + more for greasing tin

200 g (7 oz) castor (superfine) sugar

4 eggs

175 g (6 oz) plain (all-purpose) flour
+ 35 g (1¼ oz) cocoa powder
+ ½ tsp baking powder, sifted

Frosting and Decoration

1 quantity buttercream (page 11)
+ 100 g (3½ oz) dark cooking chocolate, melted

100 g (3½ oz) desiccated coconut

- Preheat oven to 150°C (300°F). Prepare a 24 x 24 x 3-cm (9½ x 9½ x 1-in) square tin. Grease tin with butter and line baking paper, then grease again. Set aside.

- With an electric mixer, whisk butter and sugar until mixture is pale in colour. Add eggs to mixture, one at a time, whisking continuously. Using a rubber spatula, gradually and gently fold flour mixture in small amounts into egg mixture until just combined. Pour mixture into prepared tin and level surface with a spoon.

- Place tin in preheated oven and bake for about 35 minutes until a skewer inserted into the centre of cake comes out clean. Remove cake from tin and leave to cool. Cut cooled cake into 3-cm (1-in) squares.

- Prepare buttercream, then mix in melted chocolate to obtain chocolate buttercream.

- Spread chocolate buttercream on top and sides of cakes, then sprinkle with desiccated coconut. Place cakes into individual paper muffin cups. Refrigerate for at least 30 minutes before serving.

coconut cake

175 g (6 oz) butter + more for greasing tin

250 g (9 oz) castor (superfine) sugar

90 g (3¹/₄ oz) desiccated coconut

125 ml (4 fl oz / ¹/₂ cup) plain yoghurt

¹/₂ tsp ground vanilla or vanilla extract

3 eggs

225 g (8 oz) plain (all-purpose) flour +
1 tsp baking powder, sifted

Desiccated coconut for sprinkling, optional

- Preheat oven to 170°C (330°F). Prepare a 23 x 13 x 7-cm (9 x 5 x 3-in) loaf tin. Grease tin with butter and line with baking paper, then grease again. Alternatively, use a 12-hole muffin tray lined with paper muffin cups. Set aside.

- With an electric mixer, whisk all ingredients together for about 3 minutes until mixture is well combined. Pour mixture into prepared tin or muffin cups until three-quarters full.

- If using a loaf tin, place in preheated oven and bake for about 55 minutes until a skewer inserted into the centre of cake comes out clean. Leave cake in tin for 10 minutes before removing to a wire rack to cool. If using muffin tray, bake for about 30 minutes until cupcakes are done. Sprinkle desiccated coconut on top of cake or cupcakes before serving, if desired.

duriancake

120 g (4^1/$_3$ oz) durian flesh

4 Tbsp milk

40 g (1^1/$_3$ oz) plain (all-purpose) flour

250 g (9 oz) butter + more for greasing tin

200 g (7 oz) castor (superfine) sugar

5 eggs

200 g (7 oz) plain (all-purpose) flour + 50 g
(1^2/$_3$ oz) corn flour (cornstarch) + ^{1}/$_2$ tsp baking
powder + ^{1}/$_4$ tsp bicarbonate of soda, sifted

- Preheat oven to 160°C (325°F). Prepare a 22-cm (8-in) diameter round tin or 2 bundt moulds about 10-cm (4-in) in diameter. If using a round tin, grease tin with butter and line with baking paper, then grease again and sprinkle with a little flour to coat. Set aside. If using bundt pans, grease with butter, then coat with a little flour.

- Blend durian flesh and milk together until smooth. Stir in 40 g (1^1/$_4$ oz) flour and mix evenly. Set aside.

- With an electric mixer, whisk butter and sugar until light and fluffy. Add eggs to mixture, one at a time, whisking continuously. Gradually add durian mixture in small amounts and stir to combine.

- Using a rubber spatula, gradually and gently fold flour mixture in small amounts into egg mixture until just combined. Pour mixture into prepared tin or fill each bundt pan until three-quarters full.

- If using a round tin, bake for about 50 minutes until a skewer inserted into the centre of cake comes out clean. Leave cake in tin for about 10 minutes before removing to a wire rack to cool. If using bundt pans, bake until cake is firm and golden brown, and a skewer inserted into the centre of cake comes out clean. Remove cake from tin and leave to cool. To unmould cake from bundt pans, invert moulds onto a wire rack and leave to cool. Gently ease cakes out of pans by loosening the sides of cake with a rubber spatula. Decorate and serve as desired.

carrotcake

Butter for greasing tin

3 eggs

225 ml (8 fl oz) cooking oil

2 Tbsp pineapple jam

150 g (5$^1/_3$ oz) brown sugar

185 g (6$^2/_3$ oz) plain (all-purpose) flour
+ 1 tsp bicarbonate of soda + $^1/_4$ tsp
salt + $^1/_4$ tsp ground mixed spices, sifted

200 g (7 oz) carrots, grated

Frosting

100 g (3$^1/_2$ oz) cream cheese

100 g (3$^1/_2$ oz) unsalted butter

125 g (4$^1/_2$ oz) icing (confectioner's) sugar

1 Tbsp lemon juice

$^1/_4$ tsp lemon zest

- Preheat oven to 150°C (300°F). Prepare a 22-cm (8$^1/_2$-in) diameter round tin or a 12-hole muffin tray. If using a round tin, grease tin with butter and line with baking paper, then grease again. Set aside. If using muffin tray, grease each mould with butter and set aside.

- In a large mixing bowl, add eggs, oil, jam and brown sugar and mix thoroughly. Add flour mixture in small batches and stir evenly using an electric mixer, whisk at low speed for about 2 minutes until well mixed. Add carrots and whisk until well mixed. Pour mixture into prepared tin or fill each muffin mould until three-quarters full.

- If using a round tin, place in preheated oven and bake for about 1 hour until a skewer inserted into the centre of cake comes out clean. Leave cake in tin for about 15 minutes before removing to a wire rack to cool. If using muffin tray, bake for about 30 minutes until cakes are done.

- Prepare frosting. Whisk all ingredients together with an electric mixer at low speed until well mixed. Spread on surface of cake or cupcakes and decorate as desired.

NOTE:

As the frosting contains cream cheese, store the carrot cake or cupcakes in airtight containers in the fridge to stop the frosting from melting and to keep the cakes fresh.

bananacake

175 g (6 oz) icing (confectioner's) sugar

150 g (5$^1/_3$ oz) butter + more for greasing tin(s)

4 egg yolks

225 g (8 oz) plain (all-purpose) flour + 1 tsp baking powder + $^1/_2$ tsp bicarbonate of soda, sifted

3 bananas (*ambon*/*medan*/*barangan*/ Cavendish), peeled, mashed and mixed with 1 Tbsp lime juice

4 egg whites, whisked until stiff peaks form

- Preheat oven to 175°C (340°F). Prepare a 24-cm (9$^1/_2$-in) diameter round tin, a 22 x 22 x 6-cm (8$^1/_2$ x 8$^1/_2$ x 2$^1/_2$-in) square tin or 2 bundt pans about 10-cm (4-in) in diameter. If using square or round tins, grease tins with butter and line with baking paper, then grease again. If using bundt pans, grease with butter, then coat with a little flour. Set aside.

- With an electric mixer, whisk sugar and butter until light and fluffy. Add egg yolks to mixture, one at a time, whisking continuously until mixture is thick and pale in colour.

- Using a rubber spatula, gradually and gently fold flour mixture and mashed bananas in alternate batches into egg yolk mixture until just combined. Mix in whisked egg whites until just combined. Pour mixture into prepared tin or fill bundt pans until three-quarters full.

- If using a round or square tin, place in preheated oven and bake for about 50 minutes until a skewer inserted into the centre of cake comes out clean. If using bundt pans, bake until cake is firm and golden brown, and a skewer inserted in the middle of cake comes out clean. Remove cake from tin and leave to cool. To unmould cake from bundt pans, invert moulds onto a wire rack and leave to cool. Gently ease cakes out of pans by loosening the sides of cake with a rubber spatula. Decorate as desired.

strawberry butterfly cupcakes

Cake

4 eggs

100 g (3½ oz) castor (superfine) sugar

¼ tsp ground vanilla or vanilla extract

125 g (4½ oz) plain (all-purpose) flour

4 Tbsp melted butter

Filling

Strawberry jam, as required

1 quantity buttercream (page 11)

- Preheat oven to 175°C (340°F). Line a 12-hole muffin tray with paper muffin cups. Set aside.

- With an electric mixer, whisk eggs, sugar and vanilla until mixture is thick and almost doubled in volume. Using a rubber spatula, gradually fold flour mixture in small amounts into egg mixture until just combined. Add melted butter and mix until well combined. Fill each paper cup with mixture until three-quarters full.

- Place tray in preheated oven and bake for about 20 minutes until cupcakes are done. Remove and leave to cool.

- To assemble butterfly cupcakes, slice a little off the top of each cupcake, then halve to form butterfly wings. Spoon ½ tsp jam into each cupcake, then position wings on cupcake. Pipe buttercream between the wings to create body of butterfly. Decorate as desired and serve.

blueberrystreuselcake

Cake

125 g (4$^1/_2$ oz) butter + more for greasing tin

200 g (7 oz) castor (superfine) sugar

1 tsp lemon zest

2 eggs

170 g (6$^1/_3$oz) cake flour + $^1/_4$ tsp baking powder + $^1/_4$ tsp bicarbonate of soda, sifted

100 ml (3$^1/_3$ fl oz / $^2/_5$ cup) milk

100 g (3$^1/_2$ oz) blueberry compote or blueberry jam

Streusel

50 g (1$^2/_3$ oz) butter

75 g (2$^2/_3$ oz) plain (all-purpose) flour

50 g (1$^2/_3$ oz) castor (superfine) sugar

- Preheat oven to 175°C (340°F). Prepare a 24 x 24 x 4-cm (9$^1/_2$ x 9$^1/_2$ x 1$^1/_2$-in) square tin. Grease tin with butter and line with baking paper, then grease again. Set aside.

- Prepare streusel. Using a fork, mix all ingredients for streusel in a bowl until grainy. Set aside.

- Prepare cake. Whisk all ingredients for cake, except compote or jam, with an electric mixer at low speed until well combined. Increase mixer speed and whisk for about 3 minutes until mixture is thick and pale in colour. Pour mixture into prepared tin and level surface with a spoon.

- Place tin in preheated oven and bake for about 20 minutes until cake is half done. Remove cake from oven and spoon blueberry compote or jam on top of cake, then sprinkle streusel over.

- Return to oven and bake for about 15 minutes until a skewer inserted into the centre of cake comes out clean. Leave cake in tin for about 10 minutes before removing to a wire rack to cool. Slice and serve as desired.

peachcake

Cake

5 eggs

125 g (4^1/$_2$ oz) castor (superfine) sugar

^{1}/$_2$ tsp lemon zest

125 g (4^1/$_2$ oz) cake flour

4 Tbsp cooking oil or melted butter + more for greasing tin

Frosting and Decoration

300 ml (10 fl oz / 1^1/$_4$ cups) whipping cream

3 Tbsp icing (confectioner's) sugar

300 g (11 oz) canned peaches, drained and sliced

1 Tbsp pistachio or other nuts of choice, coarsely chopped

- Preheat oven to 170°C (330°F). Prepare a 20-cm (8-in) square tin or a 22-cm (8^1/$_2$-in) diameter round tin. Grease tin with butter and line with baking paper, then grease again. Set aside.

- Prepare cake. Whisk eggs, sugar and lemon zest with an electric mixer until mixture is thick and pale in colour. Using a rubber spatula, gradually and gently fold flour in small amounts into egg mixture until just combined. Add cooking oil or melted butter in small amounts and mix continuously until just combined. Pour mixture into prepared tin.

- Place tin in preheated oven and bake for about 35 minutes until a skewer inserted into the centre of cake comes out clean. Remove cake from tin and leave to cool.

- Prepare frosting. With an electric mixer, whisk whipping cream and icing sugar together until mixture is thick and slightly stiff.

- To assemble cake, halve cake horizontally into 2 layers. Spread half of whipped cream over bottom layer, then arrange some peach slices on top. Place top layer of cake over and press down firmly but lightly so that they stick together. Spread remaining whipped cream all over cake. Decorate cake top with more peach slices and sprinkle on chopped pistachio or other nuts as desired. Chill before serving.

eggwhitecake

350 ml (11^{2}/$_{3}$ fl oz / 1^{1}/$_{2}$ cups) egg whites
(from 10–12 eggs)

250 g (9 oz) castor (superfine) sugar

3–4 drops yellow food colouring

250 g (9 oz) plain (all-purpose) flour

2 Tbsp rum

^{1}/$_{2}$ tsp ground vanilla or 1 tsp vanilla extract

3 Tbsp milk powder

350 g (12 oz) dried fruit, diced into 0.5-cm (^{1}/$_{4}$-in)
cubes and lightly coated with plain (all-purpose)
flour or 150 g (5^{1}/$_{3}$ oz) chocolate sprinkles

25 g (^{3}/$_{4}$ oz) butter or margarine, melted + more
for greasing tin

- Preheat oven to 170°C (330°F). Prepare a 20 x 20 x 7-cm (8 x 8 x 3-in) square tin. Grease tin with butter and line with baking paper, then grease again. Set aside.

- With an electric mixer, whisk egg whites continuously while adding castor sugar in small batches until stiff peaks form. Stir in food colouring gently.

- Using a rubber spatula, gradually and gently fold in flour, rum, vanilla extract and milk powder in alternate batches until just combined. Mix in dried fruit or chocolate sprinkles in small batches until just combined. Add melted butter or margarine and mix until just combined. Pour mixture into prepared tin.

- Place tin in preheated oven and bake for 20–25 minutes until a skewer inserted into the centre of cake comes out clean. Remove cake to a wire rack to cool before serving.

pumpkin cake

100 g (3 1/2 oz) butter, whisked until soft + more for greasing tin

150 g (5 1/3 oz) brown sugar or grated palm sugar

1 tsp vanilla extract or 1/2 tsp ground vanilla

4 egg whites

100 g (3 1/2 oz) plain (all-purpose) flour + 1/2 tsp ground cinnamon + 1/2 tsp baking powder, sifted

200 g (7 oz) steamed pumpkin, mashed

50 g (1 2/3 oz) raisins

50 g (1 2/3 oz) flaked almonds

- Preheat oven to 175°C (340°F). Prepare a 17 x 8 x 9-cm (6 1/2 x 3 x 3 1/2-in) loaf tin. Grease tin with butter, line with baking paper and grease again. Alternatively, prepare a 12-hole muffin tin and line with cupcake liners. Set aside.

- With an electric mixer, whisk butter, brown sugar or palm sugar and vanilla until mixture is thick and pale in colour. Add egg whites to mixture in small amounts, whisking continuously until combined.

- Using a rubber spatula, gradually fold in flour mixture and mashed pumpkin in alternate batches until mixture is well combined.

- Pour mixture into prepared tin and level surface. If using paper cupcake liners, fill each one until three-quarters full. Sprinkle on raisins and flaked almonds. If using a loaf tin, place in preheated oven and bake for about 40 minutes until a skewer inserted into the centre of cake comes out clean. Leave cake in tin for 5 minutes before unmoulding. Place on a wire rack to cool. If baking in muffin tray, bake for about 25 minutes until cupcakes are done.

fresh**fruit**cake

1 vanilla cake (page 33)

1 quantity buttercream (page 11)

Fresh fruit, to taste

Custard

250 ml (8 fl oz / 1 cup) milk

1 Tbsp corn flour (cornstarch)

1 Tbsp plain (all-purpose) flour

2 Tbsp castor (superfine) sugar

3 egg yolks, lightly beaten

1 Tbsp rum

Glaze

1 tsp colourless agar-agar powder + 150 ml (5^1/$_3$ fl oz) water + 2 tsp castor (superfine) sugar, boiled until powder and sugar have completely dissolved

- Prepare vanilla cake and buttercream. Set aside.

- Prepare custard. Add milk and both types of flour to a saucepan and stir constantly over low heat until mixture thickens. Stir in sugar and bring mixture to the boil. Add 1 Tbsp of this mixture to egg yolks and whisk briefly. Return egg yolk mixture to saucepan and stir to mix well. Remove from heat and leave to cool.

- While custard is cooling, stir occasionally to prevent a film from forming on surface. Stir rum in when mixture is cool.

- To assemble cake, halve cake horizontally into 2 layers. Spread custard evenly over bottom layer, then place top layer over and press down firmly but lightly so that the layers stick together. Frost cake with buttercream and arrange with fresh fruit. Brush fruit with agar-agar glaze for a glossy sheen and to set fruit in place. Chill before serving.

simplefruitcake

Butter for greasing tin

750 g (1^2/$_3$ lb) dried mixed fruit

125 ml (4 fl oz / ^{1}/$_2$ cup) water

150 g (5^1/$_3$ oz) plain (all-purpose) flour + ^{1}/$_2$ tsp
baking powder + ^{1}/$_2$ tsp bicarbonate of soda

1 tsp lemon zest

1 egg

200 ml (7 fl oz / ^{4}/$_5$ cup) sweetened condensed milk

- Preheat oven to 120°C (250°F). Prepare a round tin 20-cm (8-in) in diameter. Grease tin with butter and line with baking paper, then grease again. Set aside. Prepare a baking tray larger than the tin and line it with a thick wad of newspapers. Set aside.

- In a saucepan, combine mixed fruit and water over low heat and bring to boil for 1 minute. Transfer to a large mixing bowl and leave to cool.

- When fruit mixture is cool, add all remaining ingredients and stir with a wooden spoon until well combined. Transfer mixture to prepared tin and level surface. Place filled cake tin on newspaper-lined baking tray.

- Place in preheated oven and bake for 2–2^1/$_2$ hours until a skewer inserted into the centre of cake comes out clean. Leave cake to cool in tin.

NOTE:

As there is a lot of sugar in the dried fruit used in this recipe, the bottom of the cake has a tendency to get burnt and sticky. Lining the baking tray with a thick layer of newspapers will help to prevent this.

christmas**cake**

300 g (11 oz) butter + more for greasing tin

275 g (9 $^4/_5$ oz) icing (confectioner's) sugar

6 eggs

250 g (9 oz) plain (all-purpose) flour + 1 tsp baking powder + 1 tsp ground mixed spices, sifted

500 g (1 lb 1$^1/_2$ oz) dried mixed fruit, soaked in 200 ml (7 fl oz / $^4/_5$ cup) rum overnight, drained and lightly coated with plain (all-purpose) flour

100 g (3$^1/_2$ oz) cashew nuts, fried and coarsely chopped

Royal icing (page 12)

- Preheat oven to 180°C (350°F). Prepare a 23-cm (9-in) oval tin. Grease tin with butter and sprinkle with flour to coat. Set aside.

- With an electric mixer, whisk butter and sugar until light and fluffy. Add eggs to mixture, one at a time, whisking continuously until well combined. Using a rubber spatula, gradually fold in flour mixture in small amounts until well combined. Add cashews and mixed fruit. Mix well, then transfer to prepared tin.

- Place in preheated oven and bake for about 1 hour 15 minutes until a skewer inserted into the centre of cake comes out clean. Leave cake in tin for 10 minutes before transferring to a wire rack to cool.

- Spread royal icing on top of cake and decorate as desired.

koja cake

Butter for greasing tin

250 g (9 oz) plain (all-purpose) flour

1–2 tsp ground anise

1 tsp ground cinnamon

$^1/_4$ tsp ground cardamom, optional

$^1/_2$ tsp ground vanilla or vanilla extract, optional

3 eggs

200 g (7 oz) granulated sugar

450 ml (14 fl oz / $1^3/_4$ cups) coconut milk from
1 coconut

$1^3/_4$ Tbsp pandan extract

- Preheat oven to 180°C (350°F). Line, then grease a 15-cm (6-in) diameter round tin with butter. Set aside.

- Mix flour with anise, ground cinnamon and cardamom, if using. Set aside.

- Beat eggs with sugar and vanilla extract, if using, until thick and fluffy. Add flour mixture a little at a time in small amounts, alternating with coconut milk. Add pandan extract.

- Pour mixture into prepared tin and bake for about 1 hour until golden brown and a skewer inserted into the centre of cake comes out clean. Leave to cool before cutting.

chocolatebrownies

150 g (5 $^1/_3$ oz) butter

250 g (9 oz) castor (superfine) sugar

2 eggs

250 g (9 oz) plain (all-purpose) flour + 200 g
(7 oz) cocoa powder + $^1/_2$ tsp baking powder
+ $^1/_4$ tsp bicarbonate of soda, sifted

Icing (confectioner's) sugar for dusting,
optional

- Preheat oven to 180°C (350°F). Prepare a 9-hole muffin tray. Line with paper muffin cups. Set aside.

- With an electric mixer, whisk butter and sugar until light and fluffy. Add eggs and flour mixture in small amounts and continue to whisk at low speed until combined. Increase mixer speed and whisk for about 5 minutes until well combined. Fill each paper cup until three-quarters full.

- Place tray in preheated oven and bake for 10–12 minutes or until brownies are firm on the outside but still have soft centres. Remove from muffin tray and dust with icing sugar if desired. Serve warm.

mudcake

250 g (9 oz) unsalted butter + more for greasing tin

1 Tbsp instant coffee granules dissolved in
375 ml (12 fl oz / 1 1/2 cups) warm water,

440 g (15 1/2 oz) castor (superfine) sugar

200 g (7 oz) dark cooking chocolate, chopped

375 g (13 1/3 oz) plain (all-purpose) flour + 1/2 tsp
baking powder + 25 g (3/4 oz) cocoa powder, sifted

2 eggs

2 tsp vanilla extract

- Preheat oven to 150°C (300°F). Prepare a 22-cm (8 1/2-in) diameter round tin. Grease tin with butter and line with baking paper, then grease again. Set aside.

- In a heavy-based saucepan, melt butter over low heat. Add coffee mixture, sugar and chocolate and stir constantly over low heat until mixture turns shiny. Do not bring to boil.

- Transfer coffee-chocolate mixture into a large mixing bowl. Set aside for about 20 minutes until mixture is no longer hot but still warm. With an electric mixer, whisk coffee-chocolate mixture at low speed, then gradually add flour mixture in small batches. Continue to whisk while adding eggs, one at a time, followed by vanilla extract. Whisk until well combined. Pour mixture into prepared tin.

- Place tin in preheated oven and bake for about 1 hour 45 minutes until a skewer inserted into the centre of cake comes out clean. Leave cake in tin for 15 minutes before unmoulding. Remove to a wire rack to cool. Decorate as desired.

NOTE:

This cake's solid texture makes it a good candidate for frosting with buttercream. However, take care when unmoulding the cake fresh from the oven, as it crumbles easily. For easier handling, unmould the cake onto a lightly greased wire rack, then invert onto another wire rack to cool.

As an option, you can halve, then fill and frost the mud cake with buttercream before decorating it.

chocolatedatecake

Butter for greasing tin

Cake

6 egg whites

75 g (2²/₃ oz) castor (superfine) sugar

150 g (5¹/₃ oz) butter + 125 g (4¹/₂ oz) castor (superfine) sugar

9 egg yolks

150 g (5¹/₃ oz) plain (all-purpose) flour + 50 g (1²/₃ oz) cocoa powder + ¹/₂ tsp baking powder, sifted

100 g (3¹/₂ oz) chopped almonds/ toasted cashew nuts

100 g (3¹/₂ oz) pitted dates, chopped

Topping

Apricot/pineapple jam

250 g (9 oz) cooking chocolate + 1–2 Tbsp butter

- Preheat oven to 170°C (330°F). Prepare a 22 x 22 x 5-cm (8¹/₂ x 8¹/₂ x 2-in) square tin. Grease tin with butter and line with baking paper, then grease again. Set aside.

- Whisk egg whites continuously, while adding castor sugar in small batches until stiff peaks form. Set aside.

- With an electric mixer, whisk butter and sugar until light and fluffy. Add egg yolks to mixture, one at a time, whisking continuously until well combined. Using a rubber spatula, gradually fold flour mixture in small amounts into egg yolk mixture until well combined. Fold in egg whites in batches until well combined. Finally, put in chopped nuts and dates and mix well. Pour into prepared tin.

- Place tin in preheated oven and bake for about 50 minutes until a skewer inserted into the centre of cake comes out clean. Leave cake in tin for 15 minutes before removing to wire rack to cool.

- Melt chocolate and butter together in a bowl set over boiling water. Spread jam evenly all over cake surface, then pour melted chocolate and butter mixture onto cake and leave to set. Alternatively, pipe chocolate mixture over cake.

devil's**food**cake

Cake

125 g (4^{1}/$_{2}$ oz) butter + more for greasing tin

185 g (6^{1}/$_{2}$ oz) brown sugar or grated palm sugar

1 Tbsp instant coffee granules, dissolved in 1 Tbsp hot water

2 eggs, lightly whisked

165 g (5^{4}/$_{5}$ oz) cake flour + 60 g (2 oz) cocoa powder + 1 tsp bicarbonate of soda, sifted

185 g (6^{1}/$_{2}$ oz) plain yoghurt

1 tsp vanilla extract

Chopped nuts for sprinkling, optional

Ganache

200 g (7 oz) dark cooking chocolate, melted

200 ml (7 fl oz / ^{4}/$_{5}$ cup) whipping cream, heat but do not bring to boil

1 Tbsp unsalted butter, melted

- Preheat oven to 170°C (330°F). Prepare a 20-cm (8-in) diameter round tin. Grease tin with butter and line with baking paper, then grease again. Set aside.

- Prepare ganache. Put all ingredients for ganache in a mixing bowl and stir until well combined. Refrigerate to set ganache, but remove and stir occasionally until ganache is thick and of a spreadable consistency.

- Prepare cake. With an electric mixer, whisk butter and brown or palm sugar until light and fluffy. Add coffee and stir to mix evenly. Using a rubber spatula, gradually fold in eggs, flour mixture and yoghurt in alternate batches until mixture is well combined. Add vanilla extract and fold to mix well. Pour mixture into prepared tin.

- Place tin in preheated oven and bake for about 1 hour until a skewer inserted into the centre of cake comes out clean. Leave cake in tin for 15 minutes before removing to a wire rack to cool.

- To assemble cake, halve cake horizontally into 2 layers. Spread ganache evenly over bottom layer, then place top layer over and press down firmly but lightly so that the layers stick together. Frost cake with remaining ganache. Sprinkle with chopped nuts, if desired and serve.

sachertorte

Cake

60 g (2 oz) raspberry jam

200 g (7 oz) castor (superfine) sugar

125 g (4$^1/_2$ oz) butter + more for greasing tin

125 g (4$^1/_2$ oz) plain (all-purpose) flour + 60 g (2 oz) cocoa powder + $^1/_2$ tsp bicarbonate of soda, sifted

4 eggs, yolks and whites separated

160 g (5$^2/_3$ oz) raspberry jam, heated until warm

Ganache

4 Tbsp milk

4$^1/_4$ Tbsp whipping cream

125 g (4$^1/_2$ oz) dark cooking chocolate, melted

- Preheat oven to 170°C (330°F). Prepare a 20-cm (8-in) diameter round tin. Grease tin with butter and line with baking paper, then grease again. Set aside.

- Combine jam, sugar and butter in a saucepan and cook over low heat until sugar has dissolved. Remove and leave to cool. Transfer jam mixture to a large mixing bowl. Gradually add flour mixture and stir with a wooden spoon until combined. Add egg yolks, one at a time, stirring continuously until well combined.

- With an electric mixer, whisk egg whites until stiff peaks form. Using a rubber spatula, gradually and gently fold whipped egg whites into cake mixture until mixture is well combined. Pour mixture into prepared tin.

- Place tin in preheated oven and bake for about 50 minutes until a skewer inserted into the centre of cake comes out clean. Remove cake from tin and leave to cool on a wire rack.

- Prepare ganache. Heat milk and whipping cream over low heat until warm. Stir in melted chocolate until well mixed. Set aside.

- To assemble cake, slice cake horizontally into 3 equal layers. Spread raspberry jam over bottom and middle layers. Stack all 3 layers together and spread jam over surface of entire cake. Pour ganache onto cake and spread evenly. Leave to set, then decorate as desired.

classic**chocolate**cake

Cake

75 g (2^2/$_3$ oz) butter + more for greasing tin

100 g (3^1/$_2$ oz) dark cooking chocolate, chopped

4 eggs

100 g (3^1/$_2$ oz) castor (superfine) sugar

80 g (2^4/$_5$ oz) cake flour + 25 g (^{4}/$_5$ oz) cocoa powder + ^{1}/$_4$ tsp baking powder, sifted

Filling and Frosting

100 g (3^1/$_2$ oz) dark cooking chocolate

1 quantity buttercream (page 11)

Chocolate rice for decoration

- Prepare frosting. Melt chocolate and leave to cool a little, but keep it in liquid form. Add melted chocolate to buttercream and whisk until well mixed. Set aside.

- Preheat oven to 170°C (330°F). Prepare a 20-cm (8-in) diameter round tin. Grease tin with butter and line with baking paper, then grease again. Set aside.

- Prepare cake. Heat butter and chocolate in a heatproof bowl set over a pan of simmering water, until melted. Stir to combine. Remove bowl from pan and set aside.

- With a handheld mixer, whisk eggs and sugar in a clean heatproof bowl set over a pan of simmering water until mixture is warm. Remove bowl from heat and continue to whisk until egg mixture is thick and pale in colour. The mixture should form stiff peaks when beaters are lifted from bowl.

- Using a rubber spatula, gradually and gently fold flour mixture in small amounts into egg mixture until combined. Fold in melted chocolate-butter mixture until combined. Pour mixture into prepared tin and level surface.

- Place tin in preheated oven and bake for about 40 minutes until a skewer inserted into the centre of cake comes out clean. Remove cake from tin and leave to cool on a wire rack.

- To assemble cake, halve cake horizontally into 2 layers. Spread chocolate buttercream evenly over bottom layer, then place top layer over and press down firmly but lightly so that the layers stick together. Frost cake with remaining chocolate buttercream. Coat sides of cake with chocolate sprinkles and decorate as desired.

 blitzcake

Cake

125 g (4¹/₂ oz) butter + more for greasing tin

200 g (7 oz) castor (superfine) sugar

1 tsp orange zest

2 eggs

100 ml (3¹/₂ fl oz) milk

140 g (5 oz) cake flour + 30 g (1 oz) cocoa powder + ¹/₂ tsp baking powder + ¹/₄ tsp bicarbonate of soda, sifted

100 g (3¹/₂ oz) chocolate chips

Streusel

50 g (1²/₃ oz) butter

75 g (2²/₃ oz) plain (all-purpose) flour

50 g (1²/₃ oz) castor (superfine) sugar

- Preheat oven to 170°C (330°F). Prepare a 24 x 24 x 4-cm (9¹/₂ x 9¹/₂ x 1¹/₂-in) square tin. Grease tin with butter and line with baking paper, then grease again. Set aside.

- Prepare streusel. Using a fork, mix all ingredients for streusel in a bowl until grainy. Set aside.

- Prepare cake. Whisk all ingredients except chocolate chips with an electric mixer at low speed until well combined. Increase mixer speed and whisk for 3 minutes until mixture is thick and pale in colour. Pour mixture into prepared tin and level surface.

- Place tin in preheated oven and bake for about 20 minutes until cake is half-done. Remove from oven and sprinkle streusel and chocolate chips all over cake surface. Return to oven and bake for about 15 minutes until a skewer inserted into the centre of cake comes out clean. Leave cake in tin for about 10 minutes before removing to wire rack to cool.

battenburgcake

125 g (4^1/$_2$ oz) unsalted butter + more for greasing tins

175 g (6^1/$_5$ oz) castor (superfine) sugar

^{1}/$_2$ tsp almond extract

3 eggs

180 g (6^1/$_2$ oz) plain (all-purpose) flour, sifted

Yellow food colouring

Pink food colouring

Apricot jam

Icing (confectioner's) sugar for sprinkling

200 g (7 oz) marzipan

- Preheat oven to 170°C (330°F). Prepare two 15 x 10 x 3-cm (6 x 4 x 1-in) loaf tins. Grease tins with butter and line with baking paper, then grease again. Sprinkle with a little flour to coat. Set aside.

- With an electric mixer, whisk butter, sugar and almond extract until mixture is light and fluffy. Add eggs to mixture, one at a time, whisking continuously until well combined. Sift flour in small amounts into egg mixture and using a rubber spatula, gently fold flour into mixture until combined at each turn.

- Divide batter into 2 equal portions. Add yellow food colouring to one portion and pink food colouring to the other. Stir to mix well.

- Spoon coloured batter into separate baking tins and bake for 15–20 minutes until cakes are done. Remove from tins and leave to cool on wire racks.

- To assemble cake, remove baking paper from cakes. Using a sharp knife, trim sides of cakes to neaten edges. Cut each cake into 3 equal parts, each about 15 x 3 x 3-cm (6 x 1 x 1-in). Spread jam in between cake layers and stack together to form a pattern. Sprinkle icing sugar over cake.

- On a lightly floured work surface, roll marzipan out into a thin sheet large enough to wrap cake. Spread jam over marzipan, then place cake on marzipan and wrap cake. Neaten edges by trimming with a sharp knife. Slice and serve.

surabaya**layer**cake

Raspberry, strawberry or pineapple jam for spreading

Yellow Layer

10 egg yolks

100 g (3^1/$_2$ oz) icing (confectioner's) sugar

^{1}/$_4$ tsp ground vanilla or vanilla extract

125 g (4^1/$_2$ oz) butter, whisked until soft + more for greasing tins

50 g (1^2/$_3$ oz) cake flour + ^{1}/$_4$ tsp baking powder

Chocolate Layer

10 egg yolks

100 g (3^1/$_2$ oz) icing (confectioner's) sugar

^{1}/$_4$ tsp ground vanilla or vanilla extract

125 g (4^1/$_2$ oz) butter, whisked until soft

35 g (1^1/$_4$ oz) cake flour + 15 g (^{1}/$_2$ oz) Cocoa powder + ^{1}/$_4$ tsp bicarbonate of soda, sifted

- Preheat oven to 180°C (350°F). Prepare three 24 x 24 x 3-cm (9^1/$_2$ x 9^1/$_2$ x 1-in) square tins. Grease tins with butter and line with baking paper, then grease again. Set aside.

- Prepare yellow layer. Whisk egg yolks, sugar and vanilla with an electric mixer until mixture is thick and pale in colour. Using a rubber spatula, gently fold whisked butter into mixture until combined. Sift flour in small amounts into egg mixture and gently fold flour in until combined. Pour batter into 2 prepared tins.

- Place tins in preheated oven and bake for about 30 minutes until cakes are done. Bake separately if your oven is small. Remove cakes from tins and leave to cool on wire racks.

- Repeat steps above for chocolate layer.

- When all 3 cakes have cooled, spread jam of choice on surface of one yellow layer and on surface of chocolate layer. Stack cake layers together in alternate colours. Trim sides of cake with a sharp knife. Slice and serve.

pineapple
upside-down cake

Cake

125 g (4 1/2 oz) butter, softened

1/4 tsp salt

150 g (5 1/3 oz) castor (superfine) sugar

125 ml (4 fl oz / 1/2 cup) pineapple syrup from can

225 g (8 oz) plain (all-purpose) flour + 1/2 tsp bicarbonate of soda

1 tsp baking powder

Pineapple Layer

50 g (1 2/3 oz) butter, melted

30 g (1 oz) brown sugar or grated palm sugar

450 g (1 lb) canned pineapple rings, drained, set syrup aside for cake

6 green/red glacé cherries

- Preheat oven to 170°C (330°F). Prepare a 22-cm (8 1/2-in) diameter round tin or a 20 x 9 x 6-cm (8 x 3 1/2 x 2-in) loaf tin.

- Prepare pineapple layer. Grease tin with melted butter and sprinkle with brown or palm sugar. Cut pineapple rings to size as desired, then arrange with cherries on base of tin.

- Prepare cake. Whisk all ingredients with an electric mixer at low speed until well mixed. Increase mixer speed and whisk for about 3 minutes until mixture is pale in colour. Pour mixture into prepared tin.

- Place tin in preheated oven and bake for about 50 minutes until a skewer inserted into the centre of cake comes out clean. Leave cake in tin for 15 minutes.

- To unmould cake, slowly and gently invert tin onto a wire rack. Place another wire rack on top of cake and flip it over so that surface with pineapple rings and cherries is facing upwards. Slice and serve.

babaaurhum

Cake

250 g (9 oz) plain (all-purpose) flour

25 g ($^3/_4$ oz) castor (superfine) sugar

$^1/_2$ tsp instant yeast

3 eggs, whisked lightly

100 g (3$^1/_2$ oz) butter, whisked until soft

125 ml (4 fl oz / $^1/_2$ cup) milk

125 g (4$^1/_2$ oz) raisins, soaked overnight in 90 ml (3 fl oz / $^3/_8$ cup) rum and drained

Syrup

125 ml (4 fl oz / $^1/_2$ cup) rum

1 Tbsp lemon juice

1 tsp honey

50 g (1$^2/_3$ oz) castor (superfine) sugar + 125 ml (4 fl oz / $^1/_2$ cup) water, boiled until mixture has thickened slightly

Glaze

50 g (1$^2/_3$ oz) apricot jam + 3 Tbsp water + $^1/_2$ Tbsp sugar, heated until sugar has dissolved

- Prepare cake. Mix flour, sugar and instant yeast in a large mixing bowl. Make a hole in the centre of flour mixture, then add eggs. Mix and knead for 15–25 minutes while gradually adding softened butter and milk until dough is smooth.

- Roll dough into a ball and cover with a damp tea towel or plastic wrap. Leave to proof for 1–2 hours in a cool, dark place until doubled in volume. When dough is doubled, deflate it by punching it down. Mix in raisins and roll dough into a ball again. Cover with a damp tea towel or plastic wrap and leave to proof for 25–30 minutes or until doubled in volume .

- Deflate dough for a third and final time. Arrange dough in bundt pan or divide into equal portions among baba moulds. Cover again with a damp tea towel or plastic wrap and leave to proof for 45 minutes to 1 hour or until dough nearly reaches the top of the pan or moulds.

- Preheat oven to 180°C (350°F). Place pan or moulds into preheated oven and bake for about 15–20 minutes until done. Remove to wire rack to cool.

- Prepare syrup. Combine ingredients in a mixing bowl and stir until well combined. Set aside.

- To assemble cake, place a tray underneath wire rack. Pour syrup all over cake(s), using a brush to brush syrup on parts of the cake that the syrup does not get absorbed into. Brush glaze all over surface of cake and decorate with strawberries and sprinkle with icing sugar, if desired, before serving.

mixed spice pound cake

Cake

250 g (9 oz) butter + more for greasing tin

250 g (9 oz) castor (superfine) sugar

5 egg yolks

1 tsp lemon zest

200 g (7 oz) plain (all-purpose) flour + 25 g ($^3/_4$ oz) corn flour (cornstarch) + 1 tsp ground cinnamon + $^1/_2$ tsp ground nutmeg

4 egg whites + 2 tsp castor (superfine) sugar

Icing

75 g ($2^2/_3$ oz) icing (confectioner's) sugar, sifted

2–3 tsp lime juice

* Preheat oven to 160°C (325°F). Prepare a ring-shaped tin 24-cm (9$^1/_2$-in) in diameter. Grease tin with butter and sprinkle with a little flour to coat.

* With an electric mixer, whisk butter and sugar until pale in colour. Add egg yolks to mixture, one at a time, whisking continuously until well combined. Add lemon zest and whisk until combined. Using a rubber spatula, gradually and gently fold flour mixture in small amounts into egg mixture until combined. Set aside.

* Whisk egg whites and sugar until stiff peaks form. Gradually and gently fold egg whites into cake mixture until just combined. Pour mixture into prepared tin.

* Place tin in preheated oven and bake for about 50 minutes until a skewer inserted into the centre of cake comes out clean. Remove from tin and transfer to wire rack to cool.

* Prepare icing. Mix lime juice and icing sugar into a thick paste. Drizzle icing onto cake and decorate as desired.